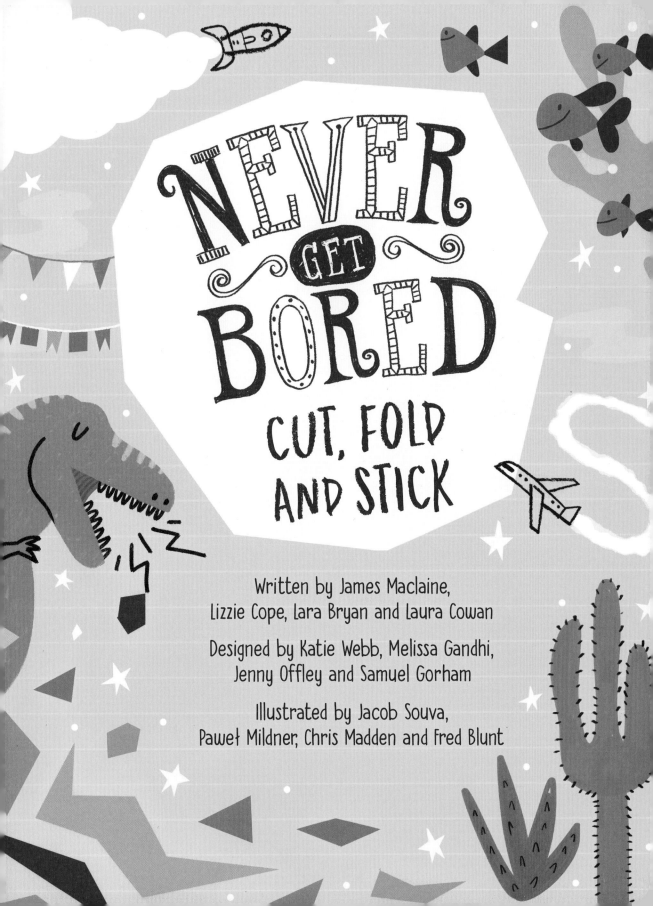

NEVER GET BORED

CUT, FOLD AND STICK

Written by James Maclaine,
Lizzie Cope, Lara Bryan and Laura Cowan

Designed by Katie Webb, Melissa Gandhi,
Jenny Offley and Samuel Gorham

Illustrated by Jacob Souva,
Paweł Mildner, Chris Madden and Fred Blunt

BORED WITH FEELING BORED?

Then, it's time to give these boredom-busting ideas a try...

1 You could make a flock of bats.

Fold a piece of paper in half, then copy this shape on top.

Pressing both sides together, cut along the line with a pair of scissors. Then, unfold the paper to reveal each bat.

Tape thread to the bats to hang them – or stick them on a window with masking tape.

You don't have to use black paper.

2 Try folding any piece of paper in half again and again, as many times as you can.

You'll find that it's almost IMPOSSIBLE to do so more than seven times – even if your paper is VERY big.

3 How about cutting out shapes and arranging them into patterns?

Overlap similar-sized circles to look like fish scales.

Stack triangles side to side...

...or point to point.

4 Reveal trails of glue.

Draw thick, wavy lines on paper using a glue stick – or a paintbrush and some craft glue.

Then, scatter salt, rice, dried lentils or sand on top.

Wait for the glue to dry before you shake away anything that isn't stuck to the paper.

5 Cut and stick different shapes, then turn them into surprising pictures with a black pen.

You could show a robot in a tutu...

...or a bear rowing a basket across the open sea.

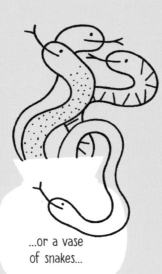

...or a vase of snakes...

AND THAT WAS ONLY TO GET YOU STARTED!

You'll discover lots more ideas throughout this book.

Just flip through the pages, open the book at random, or browse the contents on pages 4-5.

INSTEAD OF GETTING BORED...

Turn to pages 58–59 to find out how to fold origami frogs that can jump.

Discover all sorts of tricks you can do with paper on pages 13, 56–57 and 70–71.

There are ideas for 3D works of art on pages 34–35 and 80–81.

GLUE AND TAPE

Here are some tips to follow when sticking things with glue or tape – and some tricks you can use, too.

Choose your glue

For most of the activities in this book, you can use either a glue stick or liquid craft glue.

Glue sticks are better for sticking very thin paper because they're less wet.

Craft glue looks white but turns CLEAR as it dries.

Old paintbrushes are good for spreading craft glue. Wash your brush in lots of water when you've finished and leave it to dry.

You could also cut strips from cardboard to use as glue spreaders. Cardboard with a glossy surface works best.

Varnish

You can mix varnish from craft glue and water. It will protect your pictures and make them shine.

1 Squirt some craft glue into an old yogurt container.

2 Add small amounts of water. Stir the mixture with a paintbrush until it feels runny.

3 Paint a layer of varnish over your picture and wait for it to dry.

You could add a second layer of varnish to make it even more shiny.

6

Clear tape or masking tape?

Clear tape sticks to things very strongly. You can't remove it from paper and cardboard without tearing them. Masking tape can be removed, but only a short time after sticking.

End marker

After using any roll of tape, fold a small tab at the end, sticky side to sticky side. This makes it easy to find next time.

Tape ruler

It's hard to draw a STRAIGHT line around a tube. But if you need to cut the end off a cardboard tube neatly, you can use tape...

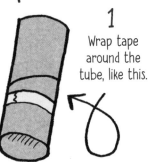

1
Wrap tape around the tube, like this.

2
Cut into the tube. STOP when you reach the far side of the tape.

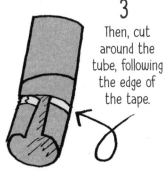

3
Then, cut around the tube, following the edge of the tape.

Labels

The non-sticky side of masking tape is easy to write on in pen or pencil, so you could tear off strips to label boxes or containers.

PAINTBRUSHES

MARBLES

Cutting copies

You can use clear tape to help you to cut out the shape of ANY picture.

1
Carefully cut around the edges of the shape.

2
Put this shape on top of some paper. Stick pieces of clear tape over all the edges.

3
Cut along the edges again, then peel away the copy.

FOLD, CUT AND UNFOLD

Be surprised by the things you can cut out –
if you fold your paper first.

Repeating chains

1

Join two pieces of paper together with tape.

2

Then, fold it in half, short end to short end, three times.

3

Draw a house on top, like this. Make sure the roof reaches the edges.

4

Cut out the shape. DON'T cut along these folds.

5 Now, open out the paper carefully, to see one house turn into a row of eight...

You could draw on windows – or decorate each house in its own style.

You only need to fold the paper TWICE in step 2, to draw and cut out four elephants.

Copy this shape in step 3 to make a gang of aliens.

Starbursts

1

Draw around a small plate on a piece of bright paper. Cut out the circle. Then, fold it in half three times.

2

Cut out different shapes around the edges. Then, undo all the folds...

To make a small star, you could draw around a bowl or mug in step 1.

Stick a small star on top of a big star.

Sitting cats

1

for each cat, fold a small rectangle of paper in half. Copy this shape next to the fold.

2

Cut along the line you drew. lay the paper flat, then fold down the head...

3

Use a black pen to draw on details.

face

Spots or stripes

legs

4

Fold your cat together again, along the middle fold, to make it stand up.

9

FOLD A PENGUIN'S BEAK

If you follow the steps below, you can turn a piece of paper into a beak-shaped snapper.

1

Fold the paper in half from the left short edge to the right. Then, fold back the top layer to the crease.

2

Turn over the paper. Fold back the top layer, then unfold.

3

Fold all four corners into the middle. Then, fold over the right side, onto the left.

4

Fold it in half from top to bottom, then unfold. Cut a short slit into the crease from the longest edge.

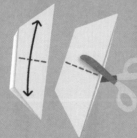

5

Fold back the top layer, either side of the slit. Press firmly.

You could draw on eyes and details along the beak.

6

Turn over the paper, to repeat step 5 on the other side.

7

Then, pull the long edges, so that the pointed parts come together.

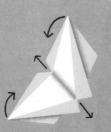

Now make it snap. Hold the paper in one hand, between your fingers and thumb, and press them together gently.

STICK STRIPS

Cut lots of strips of paper,
then stick them together in different ways.

Glue thick and thin strips diagonally, onto a big piece of paper.

You could stagger strips, up and down.

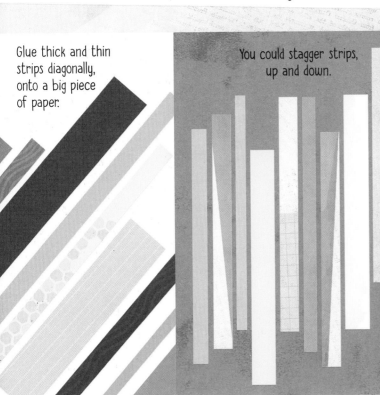

To make the shape of a tree, stick strips in size order, from top to bottom.

Add a chunky strip for its trunk.

First, glue down rows of strips to cover a piece of paper. Then, cut out a shape from it, such as this bird.

You could stick the shape onto some plain paper.

Arrange strips around a circle for a shining sun.

Make an underwater picture. Use thick, wonky strips of blue and green paper...

Add strips of foil to make it shimmer.

You could cut out shapes of sea creatures to stick on top, too.

DANGLE MINI SLOTHS

For each dangling sloth you want to make, you'll need two paper clips and some thick paper.

1 Use a black pen to draw two curves, like this.

2 Add a shape for its face and these lines for legs.

3 Draw eyes, a nose, a mouth, claws and fur. Then, fill in your picture.

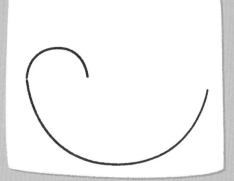

4 Cut out the sloth. Then, attach two paper clips to the back with a piece of tape.

Make sure they line up with the legs and face this way up.

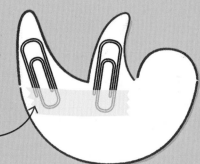

5 Now, hang up your sloth.

You could clip it to a house plant...

...or thread some string through the paper clips.

And make a monkey...

Copy these steps, from left to right, to draw a monkey. Then, cut it out and tape two paper clips behind its arms.

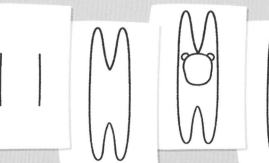

FOLD THE IMPOSSIBLE

The flap in this picture looks impossible to make. But if you follow the steps below, you'll find the solution...

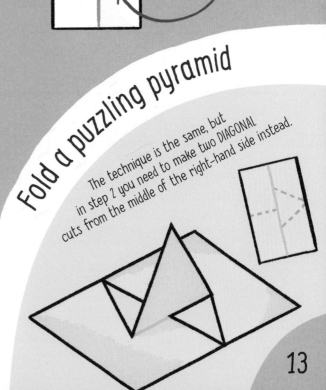

1 Fold a piece of paper in half, long side to long side, then unfold.

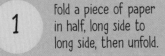

2 Cut up to the crease from the middle of the left side. Then, make two cuts from the other side.

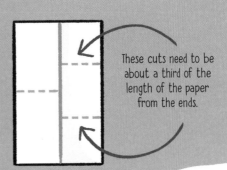

These cuts need to be about a third of the length of the paper from the ends.

3 Now fold up the middle flap on the right...

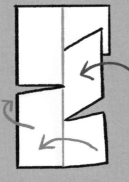

...then flip over the bottom end following the direction of the pink arrows.

4 Complete the trick by folding the flap both ways.

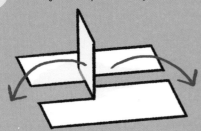

Fold a puzzling pyramid

The technique is the same, but in step 2 you need to make two DIAGONAL cuts from the middle of the right-hand side instead.

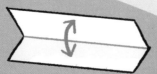

13

STICK AND PRINT FLOWERS

If you cut out shapes from different materials and stick them onto a piece of cardboard, you can use it to print pictures.

1 Choose materials for your shapes – the more types of textures they have, the better.

Packaging

Old thin sponges or scouring pads

Scraps of fabric

Bubble wrap

String

2 Cut out shapes for flowers, stems and leaves, like the ones on this page.

Crumple up small pieces of paper, too.

3 Arrange the shapes on the piece of cardboard (see right), then glue them down.

You can also stick shapes on top of shapes.

Use pieces of string for stems.

4 Now paint a layer of craft glue all over the cardboard and shapes to make them waterproof. Wait for the glue to dry.

Now print...

1

Use an old sponge to cover the top of the cardboard and all the shapes in poster paint.

2

Press the painted side carefully onto a piece of paper.

3

Slowly lift up the cardboard to reveal your picture.

The picture you print will be a mirror image of the different shapes.

You can print again and again with the same piece of cardboard. Just wait for it to dry, before you add a new layer of paint.

More printing ideas

Stick lots of round shapes on the cardboard for bubbles.

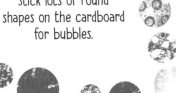

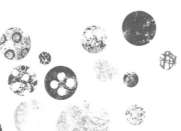

If you use a small square of cardboard, you can print a repeating pattern on the same piece of paper.

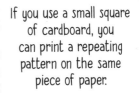

TURN JUNK MAIL INTO JEWELS

You can use unwanted junk mail, old magazines and newspapers to make all these decorative things.

Beautiful beads

To make a bead...

(1) Cut a long, narrow strip of paper.

Mark the middle of the top edge, then draw two lines with a ruler.

If your strip is very long and narrow, you'll make a chunky bead.

(2) Cut along the lines. Then, dab glue on one side of the strip, leaving about 3cm (1in) unglued at the wide end.

(3) Roll the unglued end tightly around a pencil or straw. Keep rolling until you reach the tip.

Make sure the edges are even as you roll.

Roll up straight strips of paper to make tube-shaped beads.

(4) Now, slide off the bead and wait for the glue to dry.

Bracelet

You could thread your beads onto some string, one at a time. Tie knots before and after each bead.

Then, tie another knot to join the ends of the string together.

Reuse plastic

Some junk mail comes wrapped in plastic. You could put this plastic under any paper you're gluing to protect the surface beneath it.

16

Dazzling badges

Cut out lots of different shapes...

...then stack them in piles, in size order.

To make your badges sturdier, stick them to thin cardboard, then cut around them.

Stick them together with glue when you're satisfied.

Now...

Carefully add a safety pin, so you can wear them.

Open each pin...

...then secure this part to the back of a badge with tape.

Bright garlands

You could cut out shapes to make garlands, too.

Tape them to a long piece of ribbon or string.

To make your garland stronger, glue two identical shapes, back to back, on either side of the ribbon.

17

MAKE A FLYING MACHINE

Cut a 15×15cm (6×6in) square and a 3×15cm (1×6in) strip from paper,
then fold and stick them together, to make a machine that flies.

1 Fold the square in half diagonally and unfold. Then, fold and unfold between the other two corners.

2 Make a short fold from one of the corners. Repeat this fold about four times. STOP when you reach the middle.

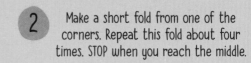

3 Curve the paper round and glue the pointed ends together, like this.

4 Next, fold the short edges of the strip together, then unfold.

Stick it on top of the join you made in step 3.

This is the front.

How to fly

Hold your machine near the front, between one finger and thumb, then throw it gently into the air.

Throw it this way.

DROP PARACHUTES

You'll need two pieces of paper for each parachute you want to make.

1 Fold one piece of paper in half, short edge to short edge, twice.

2 Open the paper, then make a short cut into each crease, like this.

3 Dab glue on the left side of the cuts, as you rotate each one to the top.

4 Tuck the other sides over the glue and stick them down.

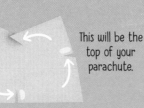

This will be the top of your parachute.

5 Next, cut four very thin strips from the long edge of the second piece of paper.

6 Glue a strip to each pointed corner, inside the top of the parachute.

7 Cut the rest of the paper from step 5 in half. Fold one of the pieces in half, short edge to short edge, four times.

Now...

Hold your parachute up high and let it go. It should float down to the ground gently.

8 Spread some glue inside the folded paper. Stick the ends of the long strips on top and fold the paper shut.

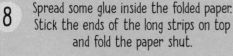

You could attach one or more paper clips to the folded paper, to make it heavier. This changes the way your parachute drifts.

19

MAKE MOUTHY MONSTERS

Fold monsters from square pieces of paper, then make them talk. You'll find instructions for turning rectangular paper into squares on page 58.

1

Fold a square in half from side to side and unfold. Then, fold from top to bottom and unfold again.

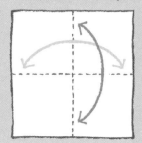

2

Next, fold the square in half diagonally, corner to corner, and unfold. Repeat with the other two corners.

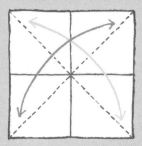

3

Fold the top right corner into the middle of the square.

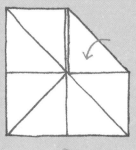

4

Fold the remaining three corners into the middle, too.

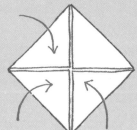

5

Turn over the paper. Fold down the top corner into the middle.

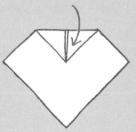

6

Then, repeat step 5 with the other three corners.

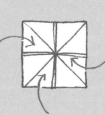

7

Fold the square in half. Draw an eye near the top right corner.

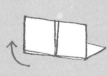

8

Turn over to draw another eye in the top left corner.

9

Slide your thumb and fingers under the four square flaps. Then, pinch them together to open and close your monster's mouth.

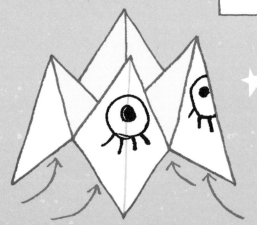

20

TURN FOIL INTO ART

Save clean pieces of kitchen foil – as well as foil lids and trays – to make your own works of art that sparkle and shine.

Reveal a robot

You'll need some cardboard, a bottle of paint or craft glue with a narrow nozzle and a big piece of foil.

1

Draw a picture on a piece of cardboard. You could copy this robot if you like.

2

Carefully squirt paint or glue along all the lines you drew. Wait for it to dry.

The lines of paint or glue need to be fairly thick.

3

Spread some more glue on the back of the foil, then place it on top of your picture. Wrap the edges of the foil behind the cardboard neatly.

4

Now if you rub the foil with your fingertips, your picture will appear.

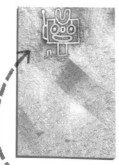

Press along all the lines.

Shiny birds...

Stick foil lids from old yogurt containers onto some paper...

...then use a permanent marker to turn them into birds.

...and a caterpillar

Overlap the lids to make a big caterpillar.

You could cut out shapes from paper for antennae, spots and legs.

You could lean them against a wall, along a shelf.

Foil frames

Different-sized foil trays can make gleaming frames for your pictures.

Cut each picture to size, then glue it inside a tray.

23

TEAR TRAILBLAZING PICTURES

Tear your way through pieces of paper,
then turn each one into an unusual picture.

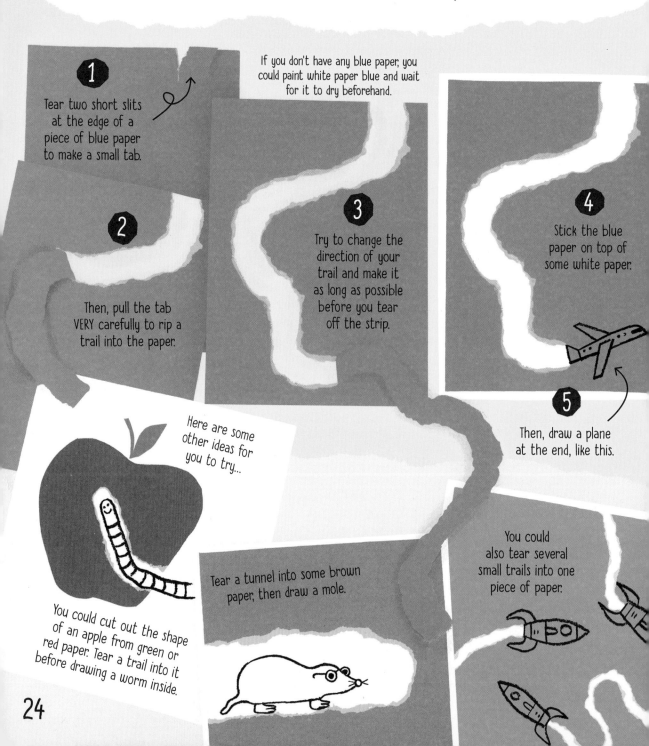

1 Tear two short slits at the edge of a piece of blue paper to make a small tab.

2 Then, pull the tab VERY carefully to rip a trail into the paper.

If you don't have any blue paper, you could paint white paper blue and wait for it to dry beforehand.

3 Try to change the direction of your trail and make it as long as possible before you tear off the strip.

4 Stick the blue paper on top of some white paper.

5 Then, draw a plane at the end, like this.

Here are some other ideas for you to try...

You could cut out the shape of an apple from green or red paper. Tear a trail into it before drawing a worm inside.

Tear a tunnel into some brown paper, then draw a mole.

You could also tear several small trails into one piece of paper.

24

TRICK YOUR EYES

Follow the steps below to create an optical illusion that makes two pictures appear at the same time.

1

Place a piece of white paper over this picture and trace over all the BLACK lines with a pen.

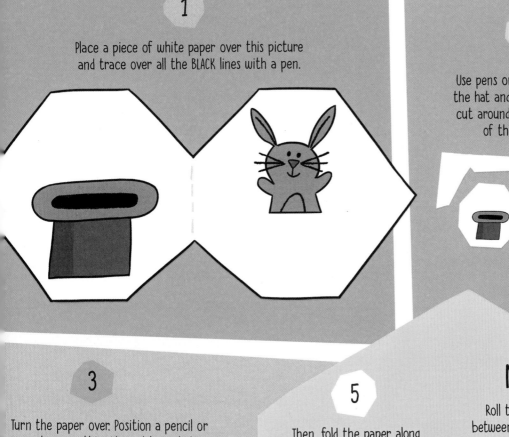

2

Use pens or pencils to fill in the hat and the rabbit. Then cut around the outer edges of the big shape.

3

Turn the paper over. Position a pencil or paper straw on this side and tape it down.

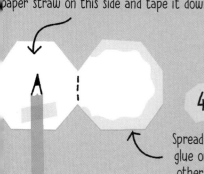

4

Spread some glue on the other side.

5

Then, fold the paper along the middle to stick the two sides together.

Now...

Roll the pencil quickly between the palms of your hands. Watch as the two pictures become one!

COIL AND CURL PAPER

Roll strips of paper into coils and curly shapes, then glue them in place to make pictures. This technique is known as quilling.

How to make a coil

 1 Cut out thin strips of paper. They need to be about as long and as wide as your little finger.

 2 Roll each strip into a coil. Let go and the shape will expand a little. Stick down the loose end with glue.

 3 Then dab a blob of glue on a piece of paper and stick your coil on top.

Now...

Take inspiration from these ideas as you arrange and glue down your paper coils. You'll need to make some other shapes, too.

Pineapple

If you pinch coils between your finger and thumb, you can squash them into leaf shapes.

Spiral

You could draw a big spiral, then stick coils on top of the line...

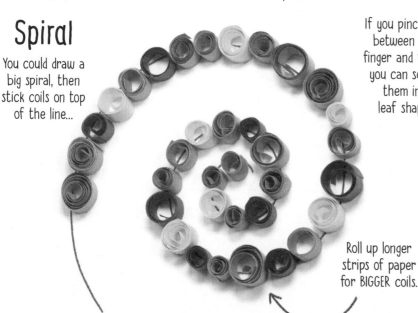

Roll up longer strips of paper for BIGGER coils.

16 yellow coils

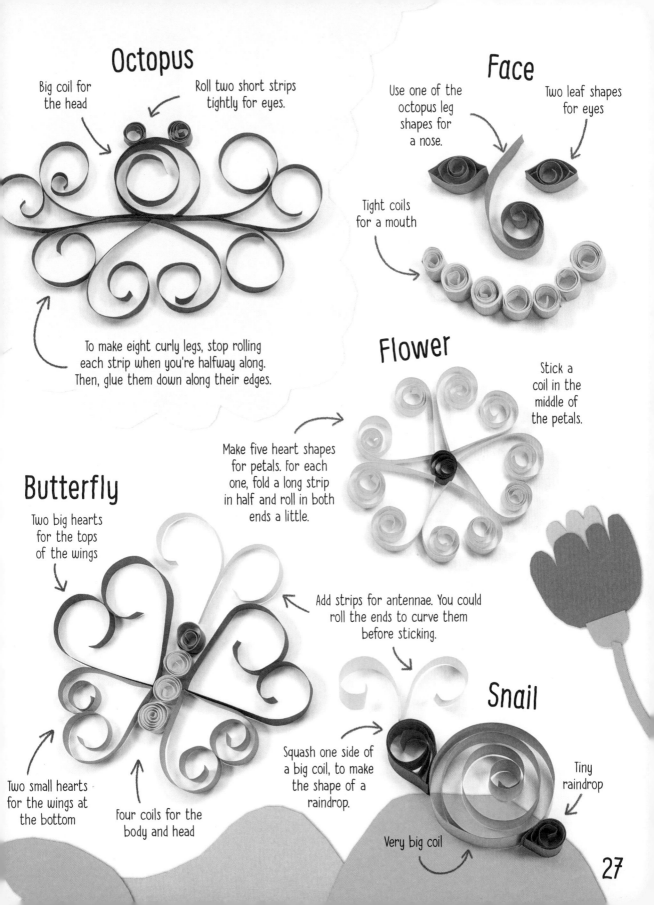

Octopus

Big coil for the head

Roll two short strips tightly for eyes.

To make eight curly legs, stop rolling each strip when you're halfway along. Then, glue them down along their edges.

Face

Use one of the octopus leg shapes for a nose.

Two leaf shapes for eyes

Tight coils for a mouth

Flower

Stick a coil in the middle of the petals.

Make five heart shapes for petals. For each one, fold a long strip in half and roll in both ends a little.

Butterfly

Two big hearts for the tops of the wings

Add strips for antennae. You could roll the ends to curve them before sticking.

Two small hearts for the wings at the bottom

Four coils for the body and head

Squash one side of a big coil, to make the shape of a raindrop.

Snail

Tiny raindrop

Very big coil

DESIGN MINI BOOKS

Fold and cut a single piece of paper, to make a little book, then stick on a cover, too.

1 Fold a piece of paper in half, short edge to short edge.

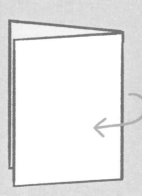

2 Fold it in half again, long edge to long edge, and once more, short edge to short edge.

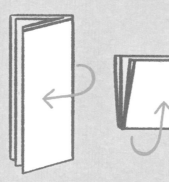

3 Undo step 2. The paper should be creased like this.

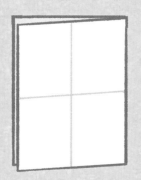

4 Carefully cut into the folded edge, along the middle crease.

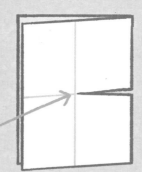

STOP here.

5 Open up the paper. Then, fold it in half, long edge to long edge.

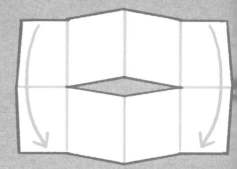

6 Pinch the two folds on either side of the slit and push them together.

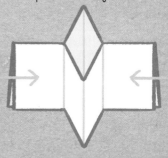

7 Then, press the paper flat into a book.

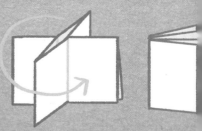

Now add a cover...

1 Cut a rectangle of thick paper, just over twice the size of your folded book.

2 Fold the rectangle in half and unfold. Then, stick the back of your book inside the back cover, like this.

...and fill your book

Decorate the cover and write – or draw – on the mini pages.

You could make patterns...

...or a list.

Bea's Book of Patterns

10 Fun Days Out

ONLY JOKING haha!

Draw a funny cover for a joke book.

Come up with a short story...

And they baked the world's biggest cake.

...or use the pages for sketching.

DAD

MAKE LANTERNS AND SOLVE RIDDLES

To celebrate the end of Chinese New Year, people hang up lanterns with riddles written inside them. You could make your own lantern from two rectangular pieces of paper.

1

First, fold a piece of paper in half, like this.

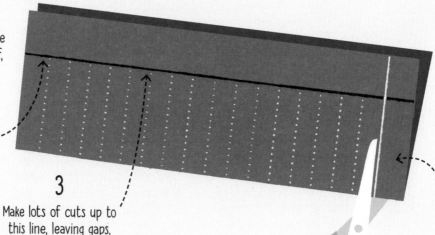

2

Draw a line about 3cm (1in) down from the open edge.

3

Make lots of cuts up to this line, leaving gaps, about 1.5cm (0.5in) wide, between them.

4

Cut off the last strip completely.

5

Then, unfold the paper.

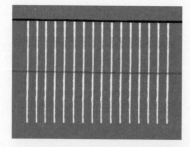

6

Take the second piece of paper and cut a strip from one of its long edges. Save this to make a handle later.

7

Spread glue along the top and bottom edges of the paper that's left over.

You could use plain paper or paper from old magazines.

8

Then, place the first piece of paper on top. Line up the long edges and press them down.

leave a gap at this end.

You could draw patterns along the top and bottom.

9

Spread some glue here...

...then join the short edges of your lantern together.

10

Now, choose one of the riddles from the list on the right and write it on the strip you saved in step 6.

What has two

What has two hands, but cannot clap?

Then stick it inside the top of your lantern for a handle.

Make sure the riddle is facing up.

Very carefully, write the answer to your riddle inside the lantern, at the bottom.

Now...

Hang up your lantern and challenge your friends to solve the riddle.

Riddles

1. What has two hands, but cannot clap?

2. What has a bank, but no money?

3. Where can you find cities and towns, but no people?

4. What has four legs, but cannot walk?

5. What has a neck, but no head?

ANSWERS
1. Clock 2. River 3. Map 4. Table 5. Bottle

Here are some more ideas for lanterns...

You could skip steps 4–9. Just stick together the short ends of the paper after step 3, before adding a handle.

To make a lantern like this one, cut the first piece of paper in half lengthways and repeat steps 1–5 on each part.

Stick on long strips of tissue paper to trail from your lanterns.

Use a small piece of paper for a mini lantern.

Then, stick them both to the second piece – one along the top and one along the bottom.

SPIN AND PLAY

If you make a spinner like the one on this page,
you can play three different games
with your friends.

1

Draw around a bowl on a piece of paper
for a circle. Then, cut it out.

2

Fold the circle in
half three times.

3

Unfold it
completely, then
draw a big dot
in the middle.

4

Draw along
the fold lines
in pen.

5

Copy the words for
different categories of
things around the edge
– one in each section.

6

Write the letters of the
alphabet, three or four in
each section.

7

Your spinner is now ready to use.
Hold a paper clip over the dot in
the middle with the point of
a pencil, like this. Then, flick
the paper clip to make it spin.

SPINNER

THINGS IN THE KITCHEN

NAMES

4-LETTER WORDS

ANIMALS

FRUIT AND VEGETABLES

THINGS IN THE GARDEN

COUNTRIES

THINGS YOU WEAR

A B C

D E F

G H I J

K L M

N O P

Q R S

T U V

W X Y Z

Now...
Play these games. They're for two or more players.

NAME GAME
RULES

Choose a category by spinning the paper clip to see where it lands. Then spin again to choose some letters.

If the paper clip points to COUNTRIES and then the letters D, E, F, the first player to shout out the name of a country beginning with one of those letters wins a point.

> DENMARK

> EGYPT

> FRANCE

Keep spinning and shouting out answers. The player with the most points after ten rounds is the winner.

WORDS WORDS WORDS
RULES

Spin the paper clip five times. Write down the letters in all the sections where the paper clip stops. How many words can you make using any of the letters only once?

OR...

What's the longest word you can make using as many of the letters as possible?

CHALLENGE RACE

To play this game, turn over your spinner. Following the creases, draw lines on the back to divide it into eight sections.

Write these different challenges in each section – or make up your own.

RULES

Flick the paper clip to choose a challenge for all the players to do. Whoever completes it first wins a point. Spin the paper clip nine – or more – times to choose challenges. The player with the most points at the end wins.

SPELL THE LETTERS IN YOUR FULL NAME BACK-TO-FRONT

FIND SOMETHING GREEN

STAND UP AND SIT DOWN x5

HOP x15

FIND SOMETHING MADE OF WOOD

FIND AN OBJECT SMALLER THAN YOUR HAND

TOUCH A WALL

CLAP x20

TURN EGG CARTONS INTO...

You can make all the things on these pages after cutting up cardboard egg cartons into different parts.

First, cut the base of an empty egg carton into cups and cones.

Save the lid to use, too.

Cones

Cups

Now make...

Animal heads

Decide whether you're going to use a cup or a cone for each creature. Then decorate it with paints or felt-tip pens.

Eagle

Add feathers, stripes or any other markings.

Lizard

You could cut out curved shapes from paper to stick on a crest of scales, ears or a tongue.

Snake

Bear

Your animals will need eyes. How about piercing yellow ones?

Cheetah

Fish

for each fish you want to make, glue two cones together at their wide ends.

Cut triangle shapes out of a third cone for its tail.

You could also cut out fin shapes from paper.

Funny faces

Use the lid of a carton for a face, then stick on different parts for eyes, noses and mouths like these...

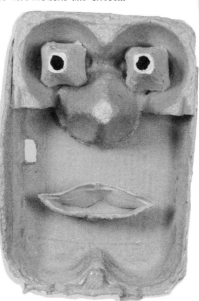

Towers

Paint, glue and stack the cups from your cartons, as high as you can.

Cheesy mice

Draw a mouse's face and some whiskers at the tip of a cone.

To make a block of cheese, cut the end off another cone and paint it yellow.

Cut out shapes for ears and find some string for a tail, then stick them all on.

35

FOLD FABULOUS FANS

At glamorous parties across Europe in the 18th century, guests waved their fans to send messages to each other without speaking. You can fold and stick your own fan, to use a secret code too.

 1 You'll need two pieces of paper for your fan. You could decorate them first...

Place both pieces end to end. Then, draw continuous patterns or paint stripes across them.

 2

Next, make a fold as wide as your thumb from one end of the first piece of paper.

 3

Then, turn over the paper and fold the first fold back on itself.

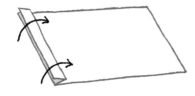

 4

Keep turning and folding the paper until it looks like this.

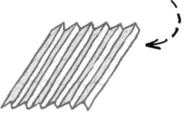

 5

Now, repeat steps 2 to 4 using the second piece of paper.

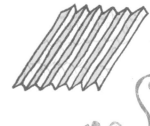

6

Then, open up both pieces of paper. On the first piece, spread some glue along the two sections, either side of the last fold.

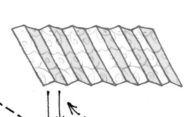

 7

Attach the second piece by placing this fold on top and pressing it down.

8 Press together all the folds. Pinch the bottom and wind some tape around it twice.

9 Carefully open up the folds at the other end to reveal your fan.

Now... Send signals to your friends by holding and moving your fan in different ways.

Touch the fan to your chin.
"Hello"

Brush the fan across your forehead.
"Are you OK?"

Hold the open fan next to your cheek.
"Yes"

Press the closed fan to your cheek.
"No"

Touch the fan with your fingertip.
"I want to talk to you"

Twirl the fan in your left hand.
"We're being watched"

Fan yourself quickly.
"Follow me"

Touch the fan to the end of your nose.
"OK"

Open and close the fan.
"Let's talk later"

Drop the fan.
"I have to go now"

Place the fan behind your head.
"Goodbye"

PLANT PAPER CACTI

Cacti are tough plants that survive in the driest of deserts. BUT these paper cacti are even hardier – you'll never have to water them.

First, find some pots

You could use old yogurt containers...

Wash and dry them first.

...or cut up the base of an egg carton into little cups.

Use poster paint to decorate them with patterns if you like.

Then, make a cactus for each one

1 Fold some thick paper in half. Draw one of these three shapes along the folded side.

If you don't have any green paper, you could paint the paper first and wait for it to dry.

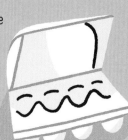

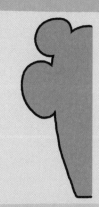

Make sure the shape is TALL enough to sit inside the pot and STILL poke out.

2 Cut along the line, then unfold the shape.

3 Draw around it twice on some more thick paper. Cut out both these shapes, too, to make three altogether.

4 Doodle dots or stripes on one side of the shapes only.

5 Fold all three shapes in half lengthways.

6 Join the three shapes together by gluing one folded side to another. Wait for the glue to dry.

Only stick the plain sides together, so the dots or stripes are on the outside.

Plant your cacti

Squirt some craft glue inside the bottom of each pot. Then, press your cactus into it.

Wait for the glue to dry.

You could fill the pot with paper pebbles as well. Cover strips of brown paper or newspaper with glue, then scrunch them up into little balls and place them inside.

CHANGE YOUR REFLECTION

If you cut out shapes from paper and stick them to a big mirror, you can transform your reflection.

You'll need to make a short loop of masking tape – sticky side out – to attach each shape to the surface of the mirror.

You could copy the shapes in these pictures – or come up with your own ideas.

Cut a dash

Top hat - - - - - >

Extravagant facial hair

Draw details on the shapes, too.

Tip: stand in front of the mirror and position the shapes around your reflection.

Broken shards

Cover parts of the mirror...

...to split up your reflection.

Magnificent mane

Arrange lots of orange, yellow and brown strips into a ring...

You could curl the ends of the strips – see page 80.

After you've added the shapes, you can move closer or further away to line up your face with them.

Grow wings

You might not be able to fly, but your reflection CAN.

DON'T leave tape stuck to glass for more than a few days. Remember to remove the pieces and clean the mirror as soon as you've finished.

CLICK CASTANETS

Castanets are pairs of instruments you play – one in each hand. They often accompany a type of Spanish dance called flamenco. You can make your own version with some cardboard and buttons or coins.

1 Cut a strip of cardboard, as long as the width of this page.

2 Tape a button or coin at each end of the strip.

3 Then, fold your strip in half.

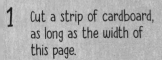
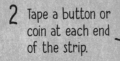
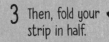

Make sure the button or coin is the same distance from the edges at both ends.

You could draw patterns on the outside of your castanets with a felt-tip pen...

...or decorate them with paper shapes that you cut out and stick on.

Now get clicking...

Hold each castanet between your fingers and thumb to click it together. Then snap away...

Try listening to music and clicking your castanets to the beat. You could even dance at the same time.

You could make big castanets with rows of coins or buttons.

CLACK

CLICK

CLICK CLACK

SLOT TOGETHER ANIMALS

You could make a set of woodland animals using the templates on these pages.

1
Put a piece of tracing paper or baking parchment over the templates you want to copy. With a pencil, draw over the black lines that show through.

2
Turn over the paper or parchment and place it on top of a piece of very thick paper or cardboard. Draw over the lines, pressing hard.

3
The pencil lines should show on the thick paper or cardboard. Cut out all the shapes you traced.

4
Cut slits into the pieces, where they're marked with dotted lines on the templates. Then, slot the pieces together.

Rabbit

legs

Did you know that a female rabbit can have up to 30 babies or kits, in a year?

Fox

Hind legs (Slot this piece in front of the tail.)

Foxes can smell things that are more than 400m (1,300ft) away.

DECORATE WITH PAPER

Whether you want to prepare for a party, or just brighten up a room, you could make lots of paper decorations and hang them up.

Rainbow chains

You'll need some red, orange, yellow, green, blue, indigo (or dark blue) and violet (or purple) paper. Alternatively, you could paint white paper and wait for it to dry.

 1 For each chain, cut seven different strips. They need to be about 2.5cm (1in) wide and 20cm (8in) long.

 2 Glue the ends of a red strip together to make a loop.

 3 Thread the orange strip through and glue its ends together.

 4 Keep threading and gluing the strips to complete your rainbow chain.

You could add more rainbow loops to make a longer chain...

...or hang several chains in a row from the top of a doorframe with tape.

Paper balls

 1 Cut four strips from the short edge of a piece of paper. Each strip needs to be about 2cm (0.75in) wide.

You could decorate them with patterns.

 2 Arrange the strips on top of each other, like this. Then, stick them in place with dabs of glue.

3 Bend up the ends of one of the strips and glue them together.

44

Stretchy garlands

1

Cut a piece of paper in half lengthways.

2

Fold one of the pieces in half, then half again, bringing the long edges together each time.

3

Snip into the paper 1.5cm (0.5in) from the end.

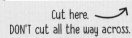

Cut here. ↘
DON'T cut all the way across.

4

Make similar-sized snips along the strip.

leave 1.5cm (0.5in) gaps between each one.

5

Then, turn the paper around. Snip into the opposite side, halfway between all the cuts you made in steps 3 and 4.

6

Now, gently unfold the paper. Pull it from either end to stretch out your garland.

It will look like this...

4

Then, bend up the other strips, one by one, and glue each one on top to make a ball.

5

Cut out a very thin strip of paper about 15cm (6in) long. Glue both ends to the top for a loop.

Now...

Hang up your decorations, or stick them up with poster tack.

OPEN A CABINET OF CURIOSITIES

In the past, wealthy people showed off collections of weird and wonderful things in a room or display case, known as a cabinet of curiosities. You could make a display of any little things you collect, too.

You'll need...

a small box such as an old shoebox

some smaller boxes or trays

glue

(You don't need the boxes' lids.)

Build a cabinet

1 Spread glue on the bases of your smaller boxes and stick them inside the shoebox to make different compartments.

2 When the glue is dry, you can stand up your cabinet and fill it with things.

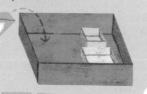

Toy skull

You could paint the boxes or line them with old wrapping paper (see below) before you stick them down.

Line the boxes

1 Put each box, one at a time, on the paper you've chosen. Draw around it.

2 Turn the box onto one of its ends. Draw around it twice.

3 Draw around the box when it's on its side twice, too.

4 Cut out the five shapes, then stick them to the sides, ends and base inside the box.

Try making a few cabinets and arranging them in a row...

You could cut out pictures and tape them to the outside of your cabinet.

How about stacking a small cabinet on top of a tall one?

Cabinets of curiosities were like mini museums. They contained artworks, archaeological finds and specimens from nature too.

What things will you put in yours?

Robots

Identify the things in your cabinet with labels. Read the instructions at the bottom of this page to help you make them.

Animals

How will you arrange your collection?

Pin badges

You could display similar items together.

Yellow things

Snail shell

Acorns

Feather

Labels

1 Draw shapes like these on thick paper.

2 Cut out the shapes and then write on descriptions.

3 Attach a label to each box with glue, or make a hole with a hole punch and thread through some string. Tie a knot, then tape the string to one of the boxes.

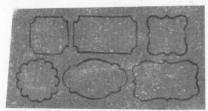

Shell

PLAY PAPER RUGBY

Discover a two-player game inspired by the rules of rugby football. First you'll need to make a mini "ball" from a piece of paper.

1

fold the paper in half, long edge to long edge. Then fold it in half again.

2

fold up the bottom left corner to meet the opposite edge.

3

fold up the triangle shape you made in step 2. Then, fold the bottom right corner to the left edge.

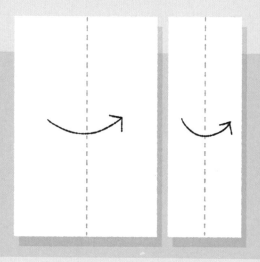

4

Cut off the top of the strip, leaving a triangle of paper.

5

Tuck the point of this triangle inside the folded sections.

This is what your "ball" should look like.

You don't need this part.

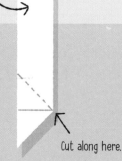

Cut along here.

Now you're ready to play...

Rules of the game

Play from opposite ends of a table.

Take turns pushing the "ball" so it slides from one end of the table to the other.

Each player is aiming to score a TRY. This means the "ball" needs to come to a stop while hanging slightly over the opponent's end.

TRY

Score 5 points for each try.

CONVERSION

Whenever you score a TRY, or your opponent knocks the "ball" off the table, you can attempt to score a CONVERSION.

First, the other player has to make goalposts with both hands, like this.

Then, your aim is to flick the "ball" through the gap between the goalposts. You can use your other hand to balance the "ball" on the table, on one end, before you flick it.

Whether you score a conversion or not, the game continues with the other player sliding the "ball" as you both compete to score the next try.

Score 2 points for each conversion.

Keep playing until someone wins by scoring 21 points.

DRAW WITH SCISSORS

How many different shapes can you cut out of paper?
You don't need to draw them first – just get cutting.

Use the shapes on this page as inspiration, then see where your scissors take you...

Apple

Keep your shapes simple. They will be easier to cut and they will look more striking.

You could cover white paper with paint and leave it to dry before you cut out the shapes.

Cactus

Shark

Swallows

Cat

Don't worry if your cut-outs look a little wonky.

Stars

French artist Henri Matisse (1869–1954) used this cut-out technique to make big works of art all over the walls of his studio in the 1940s.

Once you've cut out some shapes, arrange them on a piece of white paper and stick them down.

J'appelle ça dessiner avec des ciseaux.*

Leftover cuttings make interesting shapes too.

Try out different combinations of shapes – big and small.

*French for "I call this drawing with scissors."

MAKE PICTURES WITH HOLES

Pencils aren't just for drawing. You can also use them to punch lots of tiny holes in paper to make interesting, textured works of art.

1

Draw a simple picture, made up of lines, on a piece of paper.

Copy one of the star or planet shapes on this page if you like.

2

Put it on top of another piece of paper and put some cardboard underneath both.

Cardboard   Second piece of paper

You could secure the paper and cardboard together with masking tape at the edges.

3

Now, push a sharp pencil into the paper again and again, to make dots, along all the lines.

leave little gaps between the holes.

4

When you've finished, remove the top piece of paper, to reveal the same pattern of holes on the second piece and the cardboard, too.

If you use a piece of blue paper, you could stick it on top of some white paper, so the white shines through the holes.

BUILD WITH OLD NEWSPAPERS

Save lots of old newspapers to build all sorts of
surprisingly strong structures from rolled-up tubes.

First, make a tube...

1 Place two sheets of newspaper on top of each other. Fold in both sheets from the top, like this...

Make this fold as small as you can. This fold will help you to roll.

2 Roll up the sheets tightly together from the fold to make a tube.

Sheets of newspaper are flimsy. They're easy to scrunch with just one hand.

Rolled-up tubes are MUCH stronger.

3 Secure the tube by wrapping long pieces of tape around both ends and the middle.

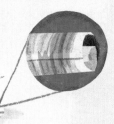

Now make LOTS more tubes so you can start building things...

Triangle

Join three tubes together at their ends with tape.

Wrap around lots of tape.

One end of each tube should be on top...

...and the other end should be underneath.

Tape another tube to each corner of your triangle. Then, join their other ends together at the top to make a...

Pyramid

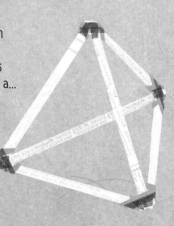

Your triangle should feel sturdier than a tube and your pyramid sturdier than the triangle.

Square

For this shape, you'll need to connect four tubes together.

Cube

For a cube, make two squares...

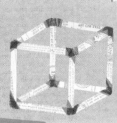

...then join them together with four more tubes.

Dome

You can make a BIG dome from 25 tubes.

1 Tape five tubes together to make this shape. It's called a pentagon.

2 Secure two tubes to each corner of your pentagon.

3 Join pairs of these tubes together to make a triangle shape at each side.

4 Ask someone to hold up the triangles, while you link their tips with five more tubes and tape.

Your dome will be a little wobbly until you've taped the last tubes together at the top. Then, it will feel strong.

5 Add the last five tubes to the corners of the pentagon shape you just made. Then, wrap tape around all their ends in the middle, to make the top of your dome.

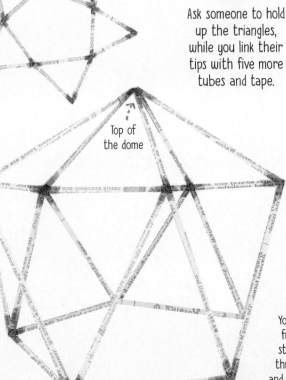

Top of the dome

You could hang a roll of tape from your dome to test its strength. Thread some string through the middle of the roll and around the top of the dome, then tie a knot.

MAKE MOSAICS

The floors of some ancient Roman buildings were decorated with intricate pictures made up of squares. These pictures are known as mosaics. Discover the techniques the Romans used before making your own mosaic pictures.

Inside a Roman workshop...

First, the artists cut pieces of stone, glass or pottery into tiny cubes, called tesserae.

They arranged the tesserae into pictures and filled in any gaps with cement.

Then, they polished the mosaic until it shone.

This mosaic was found in the Roman city of Pompeii. The words CAVE CANEM at the bottom are in Latin – the Romans' language. They mean "Beware of the dog!"

First, prepare your mosaic-making kit

1 Flip through old magazines to find the paper you want to use.

2 Cut out lots of squares, roughly the size of your thumbnail.

3 Arrange them into different piles, like the ones below.

Green

Blue

Red

Yellow

Brown

Black

Now make your picture

You could do a picture of a dog, similar to the one on page 54.

1 Draw outlines in pencil to show the different sections of your picture.

2 Choose which paper squares you'll stick where, following the lines you drew.

3 Add more and more squares to fill all the paper.

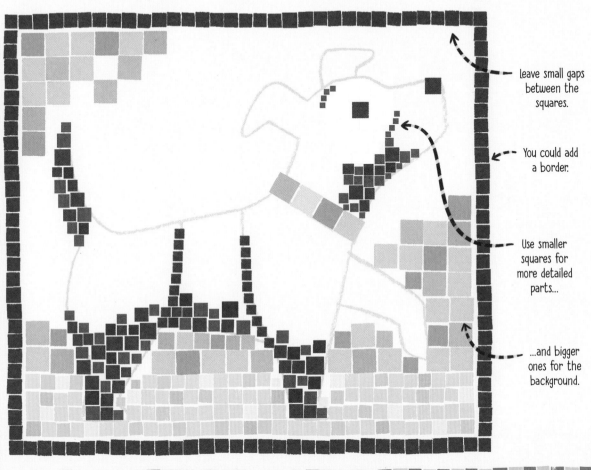

Leave small gaps between the squares.

You could add a border.

Use smaller squares for more detailed parts...

...and bigger ones for the background.

Instead of a dog mosaic, you could make...

...pictures of a fish, boat or rainbow...

...or different patterns.

DO TRICKS WITH PAPER

There are several seemingly impossible things that you can do with a piece of ordinary paper.

Step through paper

Tell your friends that you can climb THROUGH a piece of paper, then show them how – with the help of a pair of scissors...

1

Fold the paper in half, like this.

2

Starting from the fold, cut across the paper about 1.5cm (0.5in) from the bottom edge.

1.5cm (0.5in)

STOP cutting about 1.5cm (0.5in) before the right-hand side.

3

Then, cut from the right-hand side, about 1.5cm (0.5in) above the cut you made in step 2.

Stop cutting 1.5cm (0.5in) before the fold.

4

Keep cutting from alternate sides. Remember to leave similar-sized gaps between the cuts and at the end of each one.

5

Next, snip along all the folded edges EXCEPT for the last folds at the top and bottom.

DON'T cut this fold...

...and DON'T cut here.

6

Now, carefully pull the paper apart to reveal a big loop, which you can step into and lift over your head.

56

Make an infinite loop

Did you know that you can make a loop of paper that has one continuous side? It's called a Möbius strip.

1   Spread some glue on the right edge of a long, thin strip of paper.

A   C

B   D

2   Twist the strip, to stick the top left corner (A) onto the bottom right corner (D) and the bottom left corner (B) onto the top right corner (C).

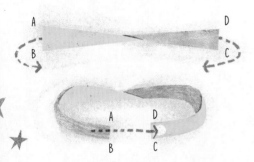

3   Press the join between your fingers and thumb to secure the loop.

You could draw a line along the middle of your loop to prove that it's infinite. Keep drawing all the way around until you reach the beginning of your line.

Can you imagine a beetle crawling around your Möbius strip?

If it kept going, it would eventually reach the place where it started.

This looks familiar...

Half and whole

You can cut your Möbius strip in half AND keep the loop whole.

1   Pinching the strip, snip into its middle with some scissors.

Snip here.

2   Then, keep cutting all the way around the middle.

This cuts the strip in half, making one BIGGER loop.

Linking loops

If you cut another Möbius strip in a different way, you can make two loops, joined together.

1   Using a ruler, draw two lines along a strip of paper to divide it into three roughly equal sections, like this.

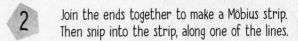

2   Join the ends together to make a Möbius strip. Then snip into the strip, along one of the lines.

3   Then, cut all the way around, following the lines. TA DA!

RACE FROGS

How to make a square

Fold origami frogs for a hopping competition. You'll need a square piece of paper for each frog.

1 Fold the top left corner of a rectangular piece of paper to the right edge, like this.

2 Use a ruler to draw a line under the triangular fold, then cut along the line.

3 Unfold the triangle to reveal a square.

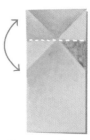

1 Fold the square in half.

2 Fold the top left corner to the opposite edge, then unfold. Do the same with the top right corner.

3 Turn over the paper. Fold down the top edge to meet the ends of the folds you made in step 2, then unfold.

4 Turn over again. Start pushing both sides into the middle, like this.

5 Then pull down the top layer and flatten it to make a triangular shape.

6 Fold up the bottom edge to meet the bottom of the triangle.

7 Fold up the left and right points of the triangle, on the top layer only, to make the legs.

8 Fold in the outer edges to meet in the middle, tucking them under the legs.

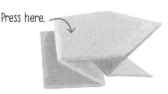

Press here.

9 Fold up the bottom edge over the legs.

10 Then, fold down the top edge to the bottom.

11 Turn over your frog. Press down on its back to make it hop.

On your marks, get set... HOP!

See how high and far your frog can hop –
or race frogs with your friends.

HIGH JUMP

Balance a ruler on top of two piles of books and see how high you can get your frog to jump.

Add books to the piles to make the jump higher each turn.

SPRINT

With one or two friends, get your frogs to hop from one end of a table to another – or along a hard floor. You could mark the start and finish line with thin strips of paper.

START

FINISH

Don't worry if your frog flips onto its back. Just turn it over and keep going.

You could write numbers on your frogs to identify them.

LONG JUMP

Use a ruler to measure how far your frog can jump each time.

Did you know that some frogs can jump 20 times their body length? That's like you jumping from one end of a tennis court to the other, in one jump!

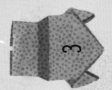

TEAR AND STICK PICTURES

If you glue down different layers of paper on top of each other, you can tear off strips to reveal what's underneath.

First...

1

look for pictures in old magazines and newspapers, then cut or tear them out. You can also use plain paper and pictures you've drawn or painted.

Appealing peelings

Around 60 years ago, several artists made pictures by sticking and tearing like this. One of these artists, Mimmo Rotella from Italy, said that he was inspired by old posters, peeling off walls in the city of Rome.

2

Stick your first layer of pictures onto a piece of cardboard. You don't need to use lots of glue or press hard. Then, stick more and more pictures on top until you have a few layers.

You could use one big picture or lots of little pictures to make each layer.

Make quick sketches on another piece of paper to help you remember the positions of the pictures in the layers.

Now...

When the glue has dried, you can start tearing off parts of the paper. Use one of your fingernails or a sharp pencil to scratch through the layers.

You can tear away big or small strips, in any direction you like.

DANGEROUS

Tear at random or use your sketches to help you to reveal the parts of the pictures you want.

Keep tearing the different layers until you're satisfied with your picture.

DESIGN A BOARD GAME

To make a board game for four players, you'll need a big piece of cardboard, lots of paper, glue, pens and a dice.

1 Make the board

Glue down blank sheets of paper to cover the cardboard first.

Then, draw around a big plate for a circle.

Use a smaller plate or a bowl to draw another circle inside.

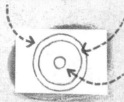

Add a small circle in the middle by drawing around a glass.

Draw lines inside this ring to divide it into 20 sections.

You could split the ring into four equal sections, then each of these into five.

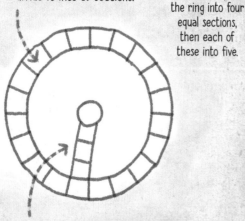

Then draw two lines from one of the sections at the bottom up to the middle circle. Add two short lines between them.

2 Come up with a theme

Choose a group of characters and something for them to collect.

Pirates searching for treasure?

Woodland animals collecting food for winter?

Monsters hunting ingredients for a feast?

3 Draw counters

Cut out four small squares of paper for counters. Draw a character or write its name on each counter.

Grubalow   Tufty   Sprouty   Sparklesnout

4 Create token cards

Fold a sheet of paper in half, short edge to short edge, four times. Open the paper, then cut along the folds to make 16 tokens. Draw or write four different things for the characters to collect.

Cactus juice   Eyeball candy   Worm stew   Spider's web

You'll need four tokens for each one.

5 Decorate the board

Copy each type of token into a different section of the ring four times. In the remaining four sections, write START in any one of them and CHANCE in the other three.

Then, add words in the middle circle to describe an endpoint for your game.

6 Make chance cards

Fold another sheet of paper in half three times, like this, to cut it into eight pieces. Write down an instruction on each one.

Move back 2 spaces.

Skip your next turn.

Hop 3 spaces clockwise.

If you have worm stew, give it to another player.

Move 1 space clockwise.

Return your eyeball candy to the pile.

Ask the player to your right for one token.

Swap a token with another player's.

START

How to play

1 Each player picks a counter and places it on START.

Everyone rolls the dice to decide who starts. The person with the highest score goes first.

2 Take turns rolling the dice and moving your counter clockwise by the number of spaces shown on the dice.

3 If you land on a token, collect a matching token card. If you land on CHANCE, turn over the top chance card and follow the instructions.

4 The first person to collect each of the four types of tokens and then reach the middle circle wins.

CHANCE CARDS

Pile the chance cards upside down.

Put the token cards in four piles.

THE MONSTERS' BANQUET HALL

CHANCE

CHANCE

CHANCE

You can only collect one token card of each kind, even if you land on the same token again.

BUILD A MARBLE RUN

You'll need a tall cardboard box and some cardboard tubes (from rolls of gift wrap or paper towels), to make a race track for marbles.

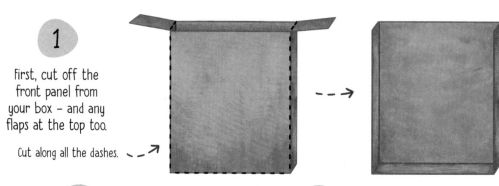

1

First, cut off the front panel from your box – and any flaps at the top too.

Cut along all the dashes.

2

If your tubes are long, cut them into short sections, like this.

Then, cut them all in half lengthways...

...along both sides.

You'll need nine pieces altogether. They don't have to be exactly the same size.

3

Now, position one of the pieces in the top left corner and one in the top right, so they slope down. Use lots of tape to stick them both to the box, like this.

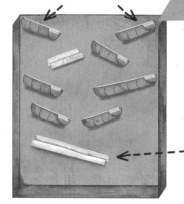

Attach six more pieces. Make sure each piece slopes down and leads to another one beneath it.

Complete the course with one last slope near the bottom.

4

Try placing a marble in the top two tubes, one at a time, to see if it rolls down the course to the bottom. If it doesn't, you might need to adjust the positions of some of the sloping pieces.

If you don't have enough tubes...

...you could cut cardboard, from a cereal box, into wide strips instead.

Fold the long edges of each strip so they meet in the middle, then open them up halfway.

Now get racing...

Place a marble in each tube at the top and let them go at the same time.

The winner is the one that reaches the bottom first!

START 1

START 2

GO!

You could draw on your marble run to decorate it.

PIT STOP

Place a plastic bowl at the bottom to catch the marbles.

Instead of marbles, you could try racing balls of poster tack.

65

CUT PICTURES INTO PIECES

Cut up pictures you've drawn, painted or found in old magazines to make new works of art – and a couple of games too.

Art apart

1 Cut a picture into three pieces.

2 Then, glue them onto some plain paper.

3 Leave small, equal gaps on either side of the middle section.

A picture made up of three parts is known as a triptych.

You could divide your picture into as many pieces as you like...

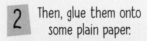

...and vary the size of the gaps.

Reassemble at random

1 Cut a picture into lots of pieces. Then, turn them all over. Shuffle them with your hands.

2 Arrange the pieces together again while they're still upside down.

This is easier to do if the pieces are the same size and shape as each other.

3 Now, turn each piece over and stick it down in the position it's in – no matter how strange your NEW picture looks.

Jigsaw race

1

Make sure the picture you use has lots of details, up to its edges.

2

Spread glue all over the back, then stick it onto some cardboard. Wait for the glue to dry.

3

Turn it over, then draw a pattern of smallish shapes on the back of the cardboard. Cut them all out.

Now time yourself and your friends to see how quickly you can each put the jigsaw pieces back together in the correct order.

Guess what?

You'll need to set up this game before you play it with two friends.

1

First, find some pictures of different objects, places, famous people or animals.

2

Using a ruler, draw lines on the back of each picture to divide it into a grid of at least twelve small rectangles. Cut along all the lines.

3

Arrange the rectangles for each picture, so they're in the correct order facing up, then turn them over.

1	2	3	4
5	6	7	8
9	10	11	12

Write a different number on the back of each rectangle.

4

Now, invite your friends to look at one of the grids and take turns picking a rectangle for you to reveal.

Number six, please!

5

The friend who chooses the rectangle each time has one guess to say who or what the complete picture might show.

1	2	3	4
5		7	8
9	10	11	12

Is it a deer?

6

Then, your friends keep taking turns to pick rectangles and make guesses. Whoever correctly identifies the most pictures first wins.

67

TRANSFORM PAPER BAGS

Save big and small paper bags to make as
many of the things on these pages as you like.

Paper bag portraits

Paint a face on each bag, or glue on shapes
for eyes, lips, ears, hair and a nose.

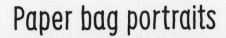

Fold back the
top of a bag to
tape it shut.

Stuff the bags
with some
scrunched-up
newspaper to
fill them out.

Try making miniature
portrait bags, too.

Venetian palaces

Cut and stick shapes for windows,
doors and balconies to similar-sized
bags. Then, arrange them in a row.

These bag-buildings look like the
palaces that line the canals of Venice.

You could cut shapes out of the bag for
windows instead. Pinch one side of the bag
together, to make a fold. Snip into this fold,
then cut out the shape.

Make sure the base
of each bag is flat so
it stands up easily.

Portable pictures

If you have a large paper bag with a handle, you could cut it open to make a folder for storing and carrying any pictures you make.

Cut down the middle of both narrow sides.

Cut off the bottom section.

Join both flat pieces together again with a long piece of masking tape on the front and the back.

Fold it together and put your pictures inside.

You could use paper clips to close the sides.

Dangling tentacles

Make mini octopus decorations. You could hang each one up by taping a piece of thread to its head.

Cut into the top half of a narrow bag eight times to make strips for tentacles.

Twist the bottom half to form its head and secure it with a rubber band.

Then, decorate it with felt-tip pens.

Trim the top corners of each bag for a pointed roof.

You could stuff the bags with scrunched-up newspaper to make them more sturdy.

Draw or paint extra details.

If you tape some thread between two bags, you could hang little flag shapes from it with paper clips.

GROW NEWSPAPER TREES

With some sheets of newspaper and a pair of scissors, you can make a tree that grows and grows and grows.

1 Cut out six big rectangles from newspaper.

They need to be the same size as each other.

2 Start making a tube by rolling up the first piece from one of the short ends.

Don't roll it too tightly.

3 STOP when you've rolled up about two thirds of the paper. Then, place the next piece of newspaper on top, slightly overlapping, like this.

4 Start rolling again to add the second piece to the tube you're making.

5 Stop when there's about one third left unrolled, then add another rectangle of newspaper.

6

Keep rolling and adding pieces of newspaper. When you use the last piece, roll all the way along.

Secure your tube with a long piece of tape at one end.

7

Then, cut into the other end of the tube four times.

Cut halfway along the tube each time. Leave equal gaps between the cuts.

8

The strips should flop open at the top. You can fan them out a little, too.

Now...

Carefully pull up the strips from the middle of the tube. Keep pulling to reveal a tower of leafy branches.

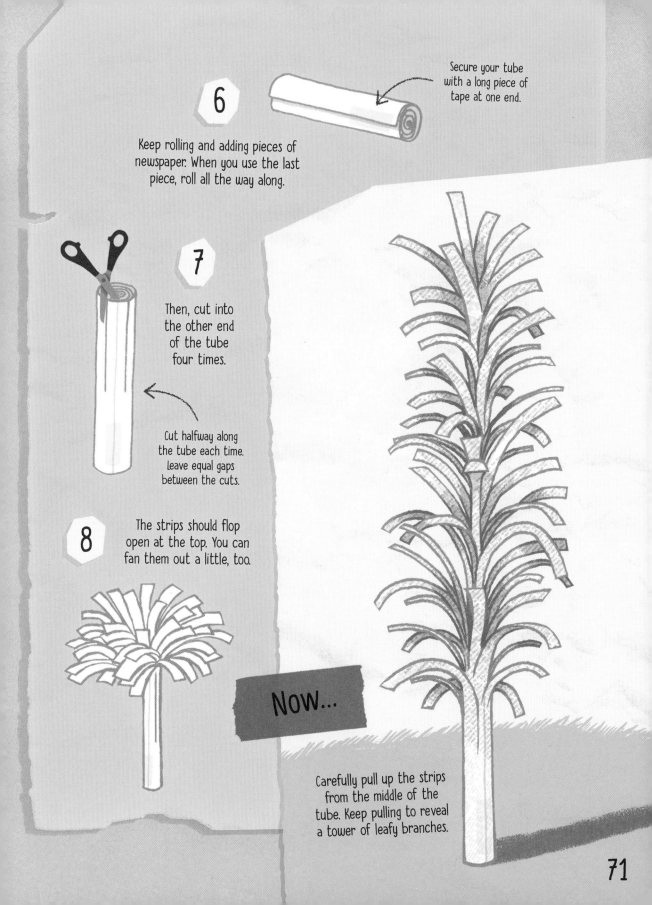

71

MAKE A MINI GOLF SET

If you turn a long cardboard tube into a golf club
and make several obstacles, you could set up
your own mini golf course.

 Club

1

First, you'll need a handle. You could use a long tube from a roll of gift wrap – or join two tubes together with tape.

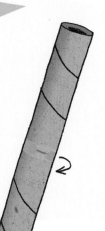

2

Then, cut out a thick strip of cardboard. Fold it in half...

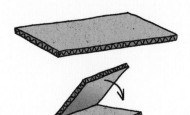

3

...and attach it to the end of your handle with lots of tape.

Obstacles

Save boxes, yogurt containers and cardboard packaging for different obstacles.

Cones

Arrange empty containers upside down.

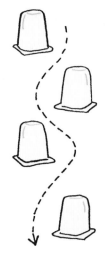

Arch

Cut out big door shapes in the front and back of a tall box.

 **Ramp**

Tape two flat pieces of cardboard at both ends of a small box.

Make sure the holes are big enough for the ball to fit through.

Tunnel

Fold two strips of cardboard a few times...

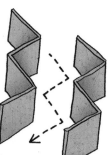

Stand each strip on one of its edges.
Place them side by side for a zigzag tunnel.

Ball

If you don't have a small, soft ball, you could roll up a pair of socks into a ball, like this...

Hole

You could place a big yogurt container or an open box on its side for each hole.

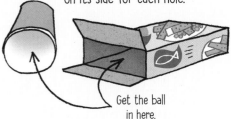

Get the ball in here.

Now play...

Decide how many holes you'll have on your course, then arrange obstacles before each one.

Try to get your ball past the obstacles and into each hole with as few hits as possible...

Tap the ball around the cones...

...through the arch...

...over the ramp...

You could use long pieces of string to mark the edges of each hole, like this.

...through the tunnel...

...and into the hole.

73

CUT OUT LETTERS AND WORDS

Countless letters and words are left forgotten in old newspapers and magazines. But you can bring some of them back to life.

Cards and signs

Fold thick paper in half for a card, then stick on words and letters for your message.

If you can find all the letters in your name, you could make a sign for your bedroom door.

HAPPY 40TH Uncle

Cut out numbers, too.

Thank you for HELPING me

WELCOME to the QUEENDOM of TaRa

Haha headlines

Find the dullest-sounding headlines in a newspaper, then cut out one or two words from each one and replace them with new words instead. The more unusual, the better!

Glue each piece of newspaper onto some plain paper, so you can write words in the gaps.

ANGER

PUBLIC GRAB SPOONS AS GOVERNMENT RAISES SOUFFLÉS

TAXES

CUSTOMER

ONE MILLIONTH MEERKA VISITS SHOP

NEW UNDERWEAR FOR BUSINESS LEADERS

RULES

Wordy art

How about making pictures that you can look at AND read?

1 First draw the outline of your picture on a piece of paper. Keep the shape simple, like the examples on this page.

2 Then, cut out words and letters to fill the shape of your picture.

You could fill a heart shape with all the things you like best.

magenta
pickles NEW YORK
CLIMBING
COMICS parks
vanilla
PUZZLES
picnics
KITES SLIME
winter POPCORN
lemonade
FIREWORKS
flying UNICORNS
singing PENGUINS
hot chocolate
swims
PANDAS
BEACHES PUGS
ICE CREAM
tennis
BOOKS
mustard
theme PARKS
cartoons nature SNOW
noodles
presents family

Choose words that describe the subject of your picture.

CUDDLY
fluffy
NAP
green
bouncy
soft
cute
CLAWS
EYES
playful
stripes whiskers
PET
paws
snooze STRetch
miaow
WHISKERS WHISKERS WHISKERS
WHISKERS WHISKERS WHISKERS
HISKERS WHISKERS WHISKERS
WHISKERS WHISKERS WHISKERS
WHISKERS WHISKERS WHISKERS
WHISKERS WHISKERS WHISKERS
tABBY
LEAP
pounce
KITTEN
sleepy agile
springy EXPLORE PROWL

You can also write on words to complete your pictures.

If you draw a star, you could include words connected with nighttime.

How about finding as many examples of the first letter in your name as you can, to fill a piece of paper?

M M m M M M
m M m m m
m M m m M
m m M m
n M M M m
M m m M M
m M M

meteor
pillow
yellow
INKY
peaceful
FOX
DAZZLE
blanket shine gleamIng
MIDNIGHT
BLACK
WARM
STAR
evening
sleep
tired owls BAT
SPARKLE BLUE STARlight
quiet moon dream BED
many
SHADOWS
comet

MAKE PUPPETS

These puppets are simple to make and fun to control.
How many ways can you get your puppets to move?

Start by preparing different body parts
for each puppet you want to make...

Head

You could draw a face or
stick a picture from a
magazine onto some thick
paper, then cut it out.

Hands and feet

Cut out small oval
shapes for hands
and feet.

Then, tape them to
the ends of the string.

Glue the face...

...at the top of the body.

Body

Use a small cardboard tube – or roll up
some thick paper and secure it with tape.

You could
decorate the
tube too if
you like.

Arms and legs

You'll need two pieces of string,
about 15cm (6in) long.

First, use a pen or sharp pencil
to poke two holes in both the
top and bottom of the body...

...then thread through the
string, like this.

Then, take control

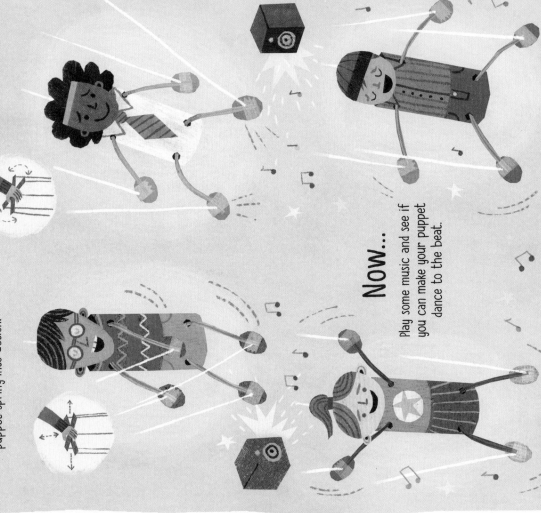

Move the handle up and down, and from side to side, to see your puppet spring into action.

Try twisting your wrist to lift each foot.

Now...

Play some music and see if you can make your puppet dance to the beat.

Add a handle

1 Cut two strips of cardboard and stick them together to make an X shape.

2 Attach five long pieces of thread to the handle – one in the middle and one at each end, like this.

3 Tape the end of the middle thread inside the tube, behind your puppet's head.

4 Attach the other four threads to the feet and hands, so they hang down straight when you hold the handle flat.

Trim the threads if they're too long.

MAKE A MOBILE

Find four short twigs on the ground outdoors to transform into a hanging mobile with some string and leaves cut out from cardboard. Follow the layout of the big picture to help you put your mobile together.

If you can't find any twigs, you could use paper straws instead.

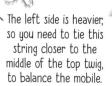

1 First, tie pieces of string to the twigs, to hang them together. Hang two twigs from the left side of the top twig and one from the right side.

Top twig →

← The left side is heavier, so you need to tie this string closer to the middle of the top twig, to balance the mobile.

2 Then, draw six leaf shapes on cardboard. Cut them all out.

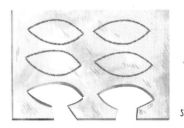

The leaves need to be similar sizes. You could draw on lines for their veins.

3 Use a hole punch, or push through a pencil, to make a hole at the top of each leaf.

4 Thread a short piece of string through each hole and tie a knot.

5 Then, hang pairs of leaves from either side of the lower three twigs. To do this, tie the other end of the short pieces of string to the twigs.

6 Now hang up your mobile. You'll need to adjust the positions of the hanging twigs and leaves to make both sides balance.

You could paint the leaves red, yellow, orange or green before you attach them to your mobile.

CUT AND STICK SURREAL PICTURES

In the first half of the 20th century, a group of artists known as the Surrealists cut and stuck weird pictures inspired by their dreams. What surreal pictures will you make?

Cut out pictures from magazines. Arrange them together before you stick them down.

You could show some fish rocketing into space...

Surreal means STRANGE.

...or put things that look the wrong size next to each other, such as a giant cat behind a row of skyscrapers.

Can you see how this cat's paw is on top of the buildings? You could overlap parts of your pictures, too.

Surrealist rules

The Surrealists came up with three rules for their pictures. Maybe they'll inspire your surreal thoughts?

Juxtaposition

– putting things that don't normally go together side by side, such as a guitar next to a tiny helicopter.

Dislocation

– placing objects in unusual situations, such as a bath, full of bubbles, in a desert.

Transformation

– changing ordinary things to make them look strange. You could stick a pigeon's head on a person's body.

MAKE PAPER SCULPTURES

Paper doesn't have to stay flat. You can cut it into different-sized strips, which you can curl, fold, cut and stick to make 3D works of art.

How to curl

You can curl strips with a pencil...

You can roll up the whole strip – or as much of it as you want to curl.

Place the pencil across the end of a strip...

...then roll the pencil to wrap the paper around it tightly.

Then, let go and take out the pencil.

You can also use a ruler to curl...

Press down firmly on the strip with the narrow edge of your ruler.

Then, pull the strip through carefully.

Fold pleats

Lots of little folds are known as pleats.

Start by making a narrow fold at one end.

Turn over the strip to make another fold, the same size as the first.

Keep turning and folding the strip as much as you want.

Gently pull both ends of the strip to reveal the pleats.

Fold then cut

Use this technique to cut out shapes, such as this star, from the middle of short, wide strips.

Fold a strip in half.

Draw a shape along the fold. Follow the line you drew with your scissors.

Then, unfold.

Now get gluing...

Arrange different strips on a big piece of paper however you want. Then, stick them in place.

Fold short flaps, called TABS, to attach your strips, so they stand up.

You can make arches by gluing tabs at both ends of a strip.

Snip a few short slits into the side of one long strip. Then, fold tabs in alternate directions and stick them down, like this.

CATCH THE WIND

Here are three different decorations to make that will flutter, whirl and spin on a breezy day.

Koi carp streamers
You will need

three cardboard tubes

pens and pencils

paper from old magazines

scissors

glue

tissue paper

six pieces of string, about 10cm (4in) long

a long stick

Koi carp fish are lucky symbols in Japan. Decorations like these are put up to celebrate a festival called Children's Day on May 5 each year.

1 Draw a big eye on either side of each tube, near the front.

2 Cut out half-circle shapes from magazines, then stick them all around the back section, so they overlap.

3 Cut tissue paper into long strips. Stick them inside the tubes at the back.

4 Make two holes at the front of each tube. Use a sharp pencil to pierce the cardboard at the top and bottom.

Did you know that koi carp swim with their mouths wide open, to help them scoop up insects and plants in the water?

5 Thread a piece of string through each hole and tie a knot. Then, tie the other ends to the stick, to attach all three fish.

Now...

Push your stick into the ground on a windy day – or wave it gently – to see the fish stream through the air.

Snake spinner

1 Put a bowl on a piece of paper and draw around it. Cut out the circle.

2 Draw a spiral shape inside the circle, like this. Then cut all the way along the line.

You could doodle on eyes – and patterns along the body.

3 Use a sharp pencil to make a hole in the middle. Thread a long piece of string through this hole.

Tie a knot underneath, to hold it in place.

Hang your spinner from a branch, so it can catch a gust and start to spin.

Pinwheel

You will need a square piece of paper (see page 58), a pin and a pencil with an eraser at the end.

1 Fold the square in half, corner to corner.

2 Fold it in half again, then unfold the square.

3 Cut along the diagonal fold lines, stopping 3cm (1in) before the middle.

4 Bend every other corner to the middle...

5 ...then carefully push a pin through them, into one side of the eraser.

Make sure the pin goes through all the layers of paper.

Hold the pencil with the pinwheel facing the wind to get it to spin. If it's not windy, try blowing on it.

DESIGN A POSTER

Share your message by making an eye-catching poster.
You could tape it to a window, to help spread the word.

First, find a big piece of paper or cardboard to decorate,
then decide which cause you'll campaign for.

ASK FOR CHANGE

SAVE THE PLANET

You could paint or write a short, memorable slogan in CAPITAL letters.

THE TIME IS ALWAYS RIGHT TO DO WHAT IS RIGHT

This quote is by Martin Luther King, Jr., who led the movement against the unfair treatment of Black people in the US, in the 1960s.

Simple shapes and images are easier to make sense of from far away.

Sometimes a picture is all you need.

Funny images can draw attention to BIG problems, such as global warming.

WIN A SCHOOL ELECTION

VOTE Layla FOR CLASS PRESiDEnt

I don't want to be a HOT DOG

You could cut out letters from newspapers.

WEAR A FLOWER GARLAND

Make a ring of flowers with just some paper and a pair of scissors.

1

Put a large plate on a big piece of paper. Then, draw around it and cut out the circle.

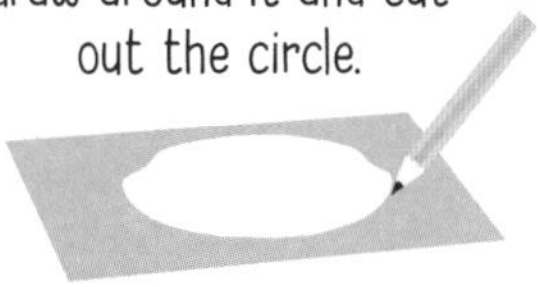

2

Fold the circle in half three times.

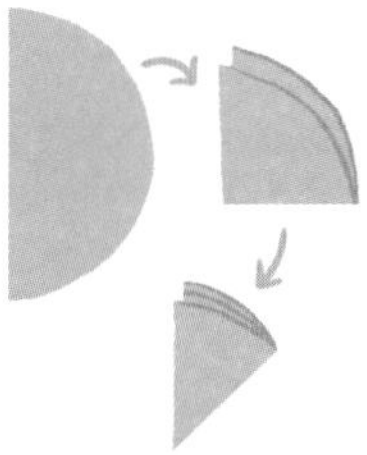

3

Draw two overlapping flower shapes at the wide end, like these...

The petals need to go right up to the edges on both sides.

4

Cut around both flower shapes. BUT keep them joined together, and DON'T cut around the tips of the petals at the folded edges.

DON'T cut here...

...here...

...or here.

5

Then, unfold the paper three times. Ta da!

Now, decorate the flowers...

Add different patterns...

...with pens or pencils.

You could balance the garland on top of your head or wear it around your neck.

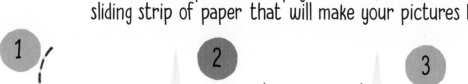

SLIDE PICTURES

Follow the steps on these pages to cut, fold and stick a
sliding strip of paper that will make your pictures MOVE.

1 Fold a piece of thick paper in half, short edge to short edge. Then, use a pencil to draw a line across the middle.

2 Bend the paper along the line to help you to snip two short slits, near the sides.

3 Cut out a long, thin rectangle around the line, between the slits you made in step 2. Remove the pencil markings with an eraser.

4 Cut two strips from another piece of thick paper.

These strips need to be wider than the rectangle you cut out in step 3.

5 Cut one of the strips in half.

6 Stick the other long strip on top of one of the short strips, like this.

Sliding ideas

Make a robot march...

...or a car drive across a bridge.

You could cut out photos to stick on your sliding strip.

7

fold up both ends of the short strip around the long strip. Pinch them together to make two flaps.

8

Poke the flaps through the rectangular hole...

9

...and then fold back the flaps.

10

Put some glue on the ends of the other short strip.

Then, stick it across the long strip, inside the paper. (Don't get ANY glue on the long strip.)

Make sure you stick this strip at the end that's furthest from the flaps.

11

Test the sliding strip to see how the flaps move across the paper when you pull and push the other end.

12

Next, draw a background for your picture around the rectangular hole.

13

You could draw a big leaf – or follow any of the ideas at the bottom of these pages.

Cut out a small picture to stick on top of the flaps. (Make sure you don't get any glue on the big piece of paper.) Now it's time to slide!

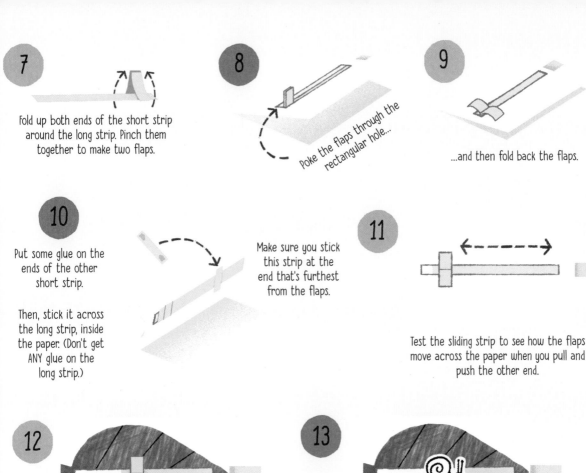

If you rotate the paper and move the sliding strip up and down, you could make a soaring hot-air balloon picture instead.

Or a cheetah speeding through the grass?

How about a bear in the mountains?

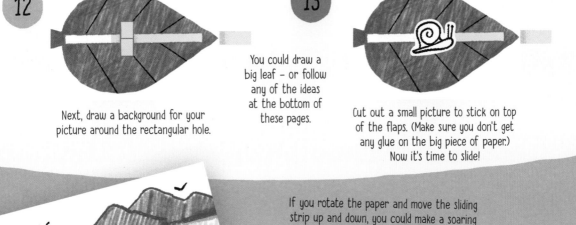

PLAY WITH PAPER CUPS

These pages are filled with all sorts of things you can make and do with some paper cups.

Targets

1 For this game, you'll need six paper cups.

You could turn the cups into aliens by cutting out shapes and sticking them on.

Write on the numbers 1–6, to show how many points each cup is worth.

2 Line up the cups on the edge of a table. You could arrange them into a pyramid...

...or two pyramids...

...or into a row.

3 Now, throw a scrunched-up ball of paper at the cups. Add up the points of all the cups you knock off the table.

See how many points you can score with one throw...

...then two throws...

...and then three throws.

Build a tiny town

Stick on shapes for windows and doors.

Tape two cups together for a taller building.

1 You could add a roof. First, draw around a mug and cut out the circle.

2 Cut across the circle to the middle.

3 Fold one edge of the slit over the other and glue it in place. Then, glue the roof on top of the cup.

Maracas

1 Half-fill a paper cup with some dried pasta, rice or seeds.

2 Place another cup on top and tape it in place all the way around...

...then shake it!

Mini crown

1 First, cut triangles out of the top for a zigzag edge.

You could decorate the sides with felt-tip pens.

2 Then, make two holes near the bottom by pushing a pencil through opposite sides.

Thread some long ribbon through the holes.

3 Now place the crown on top of your head and tie the ends of the ribbon under your chin.

What would you do if you were king or queen for a day?

Make a folded cup

You could also fold a square piece of paper (see page 58) to make a cup that's watertight.

1

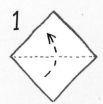

First, fold the square from one corner to another, like this.

2

Fold the bottom right corner up to the middle of the left edge.

3

Fold the bottom left corner up to the middle of the right edge.

4

Then fold the top two flaps down, one on either side.

Ball catcher

1 Tape a piece of string to the bottom of a paper cup.

The string needs to be three times longer than the height of the cup.

2 Then, scrunch a small piece of paper into a tight ball and tape it to the other end of the string.

3

Now, hold the cup in one hand. Can you swing the ball so that it lands inside?

Now, test your cup by filling it with water.

Look! No drips!

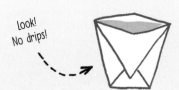

PUT ON A SHADOW SHOW

You can turn an old shoebox into a screen for projecting shadows in a few easy steps. It's perfect for playing a guessing game – or staging a shadow puppet show.

Make the screen

1 Draw a large rectangle on the base of the shoebox. (You don't need the lid.)

leave gaps at the edges, about 3cm (1in) wide.

2 Push a blunt pencil through the base, inside the rectangle, to make a big enough hole for your scissors.

3 Starting at this hole, cut out the rectangle.

4 Place the box on top of some baking parchment. Then, draw around the rectangular hole.

5 Draw another line about 1.5cm (0.5in) outside the rectangle you drew in step 4. Cut along this line.

Cut here.

6 Stick the rectangle of parchment inside the box, to cover the hole.

You could use glue or tape.

Now create shadows...

Position a shining light behind the box.

If you put something in between the two...

Turn off any other lights and close the curtains. This screen works best if you use it in a room that's dark.

...a shadow on the parchment screen will show its shape.

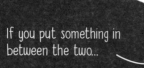

Then, play guess the shadow...

Find different objects to project onto your screen. Challenge your friends to guess what they are from the shapes of their shadows only.

Make sure your friends can't see the objects.

Is it a leaf?

A toy boat?

No! It's a tortilla chip.

...and make monster shadow puppets

1 Draw monsters on a thin piece of cardboard. You could copy these shapes.

2 Cut them all out.

3 Then, tape each monster to a pencil, to make a puppet you can easily hold.

Push a pencil through the cardboard to make holes for eyes, or to help you cut out their mouths.

You could tell a story about the monsters as you cast their shadows.

FOLD PAPER PLANES

fold paper planes, then decorate them with different designs.

First, fold a plane...

1

Fold a rectangular piece of paper in half, long edge to long edge.

2

fold up the bottom right corner of the top layer to the middle.

3

fold this flap over to the middle again.

4

Fold it one last time.

HURRICANE HAWK

PELICAN JET

Write a name for your plane on one of its wings.

STAR SURFER

FLYING ARROW

RAINBOW CHASER

How to decorate it

Use pencils or felt-tip pens to decorate your plane. Here are some ideas to get you started.

Doodle patterns on the wings.

Arrows

Feathers

STAR SURFER

LB.

Rainbow

Racing stripes

Stars

Draw circles for windows on the side of your plane, then show who's on board.

5

Turn the piece of paper over.

6

Repeat steps 2 to 4 on this side, from the bottom left corner.

7

Open up the wings. Your plane is now ready to customize.

You could turn your plane into a flying animal. Draw on eyes and other markings.

SWAN JET

Wavy wings

Two eyes inside teardrop shapes

Curved beak with two dots

THE FLYING FISH

Long, narrow body

Two eyes

Shapes for its fins and tail

DRAGONFLYER

Round shapes for the head and top two segments of the body

Long, thin shape, divided by lines

Pair of wings on either side, filled with little dots

You could make up a logo for your plane, such as...

...a shooting star...

LB.

...a flag...

...or a design based on your initials.

Now take flight...

To launch your plane, hold it just in front of the middle and... throw!

AND IF YOU'RE STILL BORED...

Cut out hand-shaped jellyfish

If you draw around your hand several times and cut out the shapes you make, you can turn each one into a jellyfish, like this...

Make paper clip birds

Cut out bird shapes and decorate them with pens.

Then, make feet for each bird...

Unfold two paper clips and join them together with tape, like this.

Use more tape to attach them to the back.

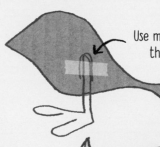

Unfold without touching

For this trick, you'll need a plate, with a shallow layer of water on it.

1 Place a thin piece of paper on top of this sun shape. Draw over all the black lines.

2 Cut out the shape. Then, fold each of the triangular points into the middle.

3 Gently place the folded shape on the water. Shout "Open sesame!" if you like — and watch it open up.

94

Play pick it up

This is a game for two or more players. Each player will need two sheets of paper, a paper straw and a bowl.

1 Cut each of your sheets into nine rectangles for tokens. Write your initials on them.

2 Scatter all the tokens on top of a table, with the initials facing up.

3 Players suck their straws to pick up their tokens, then move them to their bowls as quickly as they can.

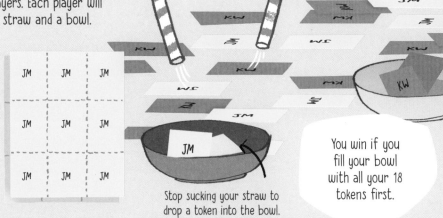

Stop sucking your straw to drop a token into the bowl.

You win if you fill your bowl with all your 18 tokens first.

Turn glue into decorations

Create shapes by spreading a thick layer of white craft glue on some foil.

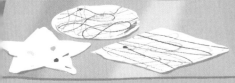

Drip a few drops of food dye into the glue. Then, make swirly patterns with a thin stick or the tip of a pencil.

When the glue has dried solid and clear, you can cut out the shapes neatly...

...and tape on some ribbon to hang them up.

Open a picture gallery

Choose pictures or photos to cut out. Stick them on paper, then doodle a different frame around each one.

And blow a paper horn

Roll up a piece of paper into a cone, then secure it with tape.

Snip off the end and blow into this hole.

HONKK

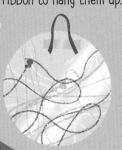

VISIT USBORNE QUICKLINKS

There are EVEN MORE cutting, folding and sticking ideas on the internet, but they're hidden among lots of boring stuff. For links to fun and inspiring websites, go to Usborne Quicklinks at usborne.com/Quicklinks and type in the title of this book.

You'll find links to websites where you can...

Cut out shapes that slot together

Build sculptures from recycling

Fold an origami helmet

And turn milk into glue

Please follow the internet safety guidelines at Usborne Quicklinks. Children should be supervised online.

Usborne Publishing is not responsible and does not accept liability for the availability or content of any website other than its own, or for any exposure to harmful, offensive or inaccurate material which may appear on the Web. Usborne Publishing will have no liability for any damage or loss caused by viruses that may be downloaded as a result of browsing the sites it recommends.

Additional writing by
Jordan Akpojaro

Series editor: Jane Chisholm

Additional illustrations by
Nat Hues, Klas Fahlén,
Danielle Kroll and
Bethany Christou

Additional design by
Freya Harrison
and Vickie Robinson

Series designer: Stephen Moncrieff

Photographs on p6 © Yurij Omelchenko/Shutterstock; p7 © Eric Isselee/Shutterstock; p23 © Winai Tepsuttinun/Dreamstime.com, © Alekseykolotvin28/Dreamstime.com, © Wichien Tepsuttinun/Dreamstime.com; p54 © colaimages/Alamy Stock Photo; pp60–61 © Aleksey Stiop/Dreamstime.com, © Simon Thomas/Dreamstime.com, © Olgers1/Dreamstime.com; p66 © Andrew Kazmierski/Dreamstime.com; p67 © Seadam/Dreamstime.com; © Agami Photo Agency/Dreamstime.com, © Rgbe/Dreamstime.com; p79 © Ekaterina Pereslavtseva/Dreamstime.com, © Jakkapan Jabjainai/Dreamstime.com, © Iakov Kalinin/Dreamstime.com, © Khatawut Chaemchamras/Dreamstime.com; p86 © Radu Razvan Gheorghe/Dreamstime.com; p87 © Sergey Uryadnikov/Shutterstock, © Slowmotiongli/Dreamstime.com; p95 © Karel Cerny/Shutterstock, © KENTA SUDO/Shutterstock, © Anna_Pustynnikova/Shutterstock